The Complete Crock Pot Cookbook

2000+ Days of Super Simple, Quick and Economical Recipes for Beginners | Explore the Delicious Flavors of Slow Cooking on a Budget

Kate Williams

TABLE OF CONTENTS

INTRODUCTION

"A Crock-Pot, sometimes just referred to as a Crock-Pot, is a cooking appliance that can be used instead of a regular stovetop to prepare food. A unique type of pot is a crock-pot. In some circles, this particular type of pot is also known as a crock pot. The crock-pot has an AC outlet, a high setting, and a low setting, but it doesn't have any other temperature settings besides high and low. This is because a Crock-Pot will gradually increase in temperature over the course of a prolonged cooking time, at which point it will turn itself off. This is because over the course of a lengthy cooking period, the temperature in a Crock-Pot will gradually rise. The Crock-Pot is a particular type of crock-pot that enables the cook to leave the kitchen while the meal is being prepared. This means that you can prepare the entire dinner in the slow cooker in the morning before leaving for work, and it will be prepared by the time you return from work, which will be between eight and ten hours later.

The slow-cooking method ensures that the foods cooked in Crock-Pots retain their natural fluids and flavors because of the device's design, which eliminates the need for preheating. Preheating is not necessary for Crock-Pots. A Crock-Pot does not require any preheating before use. A Crock-Pot can be used to cook a wide variety of foods, including meats that have been frozen. Add one cup (235 ml) of heated liquid to the pot first, and then add another four to six hours—or two hours—of cooking time, depending on whether you're using the low or high setting. You will need to simmer the food for an additional two hours if you are using the high setting. If you decide to prepare your food slowly, cooking will take between four and six hours.

There are two different roasting times you can select from: a traditional roast will finish in about ten to twelve hours on low, or a quicker roast may finish in about six to eight hours on high. As the end of the cooking process approaches, you should check the temperature using a thermometer designed specifically for use with meat in order to determine the internal temperature of the flesh. The time has come for you to cook as the process is coming to an end. While chicken should be cooked to an internal temperature of at least 180 degrees Fahrenheit, beef and pig should be cooked to an internal temperature between 71 and 77 degrees Celsius (between 160 and 170 degrees) (82 degrees Celsius). Even though browning the meat is not required before placing it in a slow cooker, you should pre-cook extremely fatty slices of meat to help reduce the amount of extra fat before doing so. It is not necessary to brown the meat before adding it to a slow cooker. Once you've finished using this technique, you won't have any trouble inserting the meat into the slow cooker.

Pasta should be cooked according to the standard procedure, which is to cook it in water that is rapidly boiling until it is al dente, before being added to the Crock-Pot for the last 30 minutes of cooking, if pasta is to be included in the recipe. Pasta should first be made using the traditional method before being added to the recipe. If you want to include pasta in the dish, you must first prepare it according to tradition. If you want to serve pasta for dinner, you should first prepare it using the traditional method, which is to cook it in rapidly boiling water until it is sufficiently chewy. Pasta should first be made using the standard method if you intend to include it in the meal. If you want to include pasta in the recipe, you must first prepare the pasta according to the usual method.

After a long day at work, dinner might already be prepared in the slow cooker and ready for you to enjoy when you get home. In addition to being scalding hot, it will also be bursting with flavor and aroma, and it will have been painstakingly prepared according to your preferences for both the dish's temperature and ingredients. This is made possible by the fact that using a Crock-Pot to cook food is a fantastic and dependable method that does not require the cook to closely monitor the cooking process. The process is safer and the chef's time is freed up as a result. The process becomes more efficient overall because the chef has more time to devote to other tasks as a result."

CHAPTER 1
CROCKPOT

The slow cooker, also referred to as a crock-pot, is an electrical cooking appliance that rests on top of a countertop and simmers food at a lower temperature than other cooking methods like baking, boiling, and frying. This enables you to boil a variety of foods without having to pay close attention to the cooking for a long time, including pot roast, soups, stews, and other dishes (such as drinks, desserts, and dips).

- **The best ways to put a slow cooker to use**

To get started, you will need to make sure that each of the components is ready to go.

- Make sure to cut each ingredient into pieces that are the same size if your recipe calls for slicing meat or chopping vegetables. By doing this, the ingredients will all cook at the same rate.
- You should proceed to the third step after completing the second step, which entails packing the internal pot with all of your ingredients and covering it with the lid.
- If a recipe calls for both meat and vegetables, layer the vegetables in the bottom of your slow cooker first, followed by the meat. The meat will cook evenly as a result of this. This is because cooking time for vegetables typically takes a lot longer than

it does for meat. While it's important to fill your slow cooker at least two thirds of the way, you shouldn't ever fill it any more than that during the cooking process. This will guarantee that the meal's temperature stays constant while it cooks.

- If your device has a lid lock, use it to make sure the lid is always securely fastened and cannot be removed.
- The instructions that came with your recipe should be followed in order to determine how long the food will need to cook for and what temperature the slow cooker should be set to after you have finished plugging it in.
- If you need to cook something quickly, you can set the temperature to high. If you need the food to cook slowly over the course of the day, you can set the temperature to low. The time it takes to cook food is reduced by half when using the high setting as opposed to the low setting, which is what would happen when using the low setting. It will be your responsibility to independently set a timer if the slow cooker you are using does not already have one.
- The way that roast ovens are used in the kitchen is similar to how slow cookers are used. To properly prepare some types of food, the roast oven must first be heated up. Before making changes to the device's settings, you must first immerse the portable sous vide crock-Pot in a pot of water with an airtight container containing the ingredients. You will be able to modify the settings on the portable sous vide crock-Pot after completing this step.
- Unless the cooker has a setting that enables it to do this automatically, you will need to manually turn off the cooker or use the option to keep the food warm in the event that the meal is finished before the cooker.
- It's helpful to be aware that the majority of electric slow cookers, also referred to as crock pots, can be heated similarly to roasting ovens. This particular piece of information is widely available. To make sure that it is not kept at a temperature that is too low for a prolonged period, test it out on some meat and poultry.

HOW DOES IT FUNCTION?

"The parts consist of a base with a heating element, a glass cover, and a container for the liquid. The start of the cooking process is signaled by placing the food in the cooking vessel. It is frequently built out of substantial stoneware because it maintains a constant temperature throughout.

The meal is prepared in a way that is comparable to cooking it on a stovetop or in a Dutch oven, depending on the technique that is used. A crock-pot, on the other hand, starts by heating the bottom of the pot, then continues by heating the sides of the pot, and finally finishes by cooking the food. You can be sure that the heat will be distributed evenly throughout the entire pot by employing this method. The steam will rise to the surface due to the heat, which will cause the lid to pull away from the pot and create a vacuum between the lid and the pot. The best way to prevent food from losing moisture content while it is being prepared is to maintain a low, constant temperature throughout the cooking process. Either the liquid will not evaporate or concentrate, or neither of these processes will result in any volume loss."

- **CROCKPOT SETTINGS**

The majority of devices can be set to one of three different levels: low, high, or heated. In a crock-pot, the temperature can be changed between 175 and 215 degrees Fahrenheit (F). 215 degrees Fahrenheit is the highest temperature that can be achieved using either the low or high setting. Whatever setting is being used, this is true. On the other hand, choosing the low setting will result in more times when the temperature is turned on and off. Using the high setting will enable the food to be cooked more quickly than using the low option due to the higher temperature. This is a result of the prolonged cooking process. When the warm setting is activated, the internal temperature of the Crock-Pot will range from 165 to 175 degrees Fahrenheit, depending on how high the setting is turned.

- Depending on your preferences, you can use either the low or high temperature setting for large roasts.
- Healthy proteins Try cooking bone-in chicken breasts, thighs, or pork loin for an extended period over a low fire. This will produce a dinner that is satisfying as well as tasty.
- Depending on how quickly you want the food to cook, you can use either the low or high setting when making a casserole or soup.
- Warm temperatures are ideal for maintaining food's temperature while it is being served at social gatherings.
- use of a slow cooker can lead to a number of advantages
- Customers who use the slow cooker may benefit in a variety of ways from doing so.

This low-wattage appliance uses a lot less power than blasting your oven or cooktop for several hours straight, which is good news for your wallet. Additionally, it is a risk-free method of cooking in a small space that fills the house with the aroma of something delicious while not heating the entire thing.

Delicate Meats By gently braising them for a long time over a low fire, even the toughest cuts of beef can become tender. Braising is the name of this technique. Making your own meals at home will allow you to spend less money on food than going to expensive restaurants, where the preparation may take a full day.

Even though many of us would like to spend more time cooking, due to everyone's busy schedules, we simply do not have the time to do so. We have a lot more time to devote to other tasks that are equally important or more important when we use slow cooking as a method for the preparation of meals that can be "set and forget." Additionally, the preparation of the ingredients before adding them to the slow cooker can be characterized as having a relatively low level of complexity.

A variety of cooking techniques can be used to create recipes for low-fat meals that can be made in a slow cooker, including poaching and braising the meat, cooking it in broths or water, adding spices and other aromatics, and a number of other techniques. Food prepared using these techniques has a higher nutrient density than other types of food.

CHAPTER 2:
BENEFITS OF SLOW COOKER

1. Hassle-free cooking

"There is an old proverb that states that a pot that is constantly being watched will never boil; this proverb is especially relevant to slow cookers. With a slow cooker, all you have to do is add your ingredients, set the temperature, and then leave the kitchen. This requires very little "watching" on your part. That represents the height of what can be done in the kitchen quickly. When you return later, all of the ingredients you added will have combined to produce a dish that will make your salivary glands tingle.

2. Slow cooker magic

Because slow cookers cook at such low temperatures, flavors can penetrate the food very gradually, creating a final flavor that is much more robust and aromatic and is evenly distributed throughout the entire cooker's contents. This is because the slow cookers' low cooking temperatures allow the flavors to permeate the food.

For making spicy and flavorful meals like stews, casseroles, and chilis, people often use a slow cooker. One of the factors influencing people's decision to use the slow cooker for these kinds of dishes is this feature.

3. Tender meat

Slow cookers frequently require a sizable amount of liquid in order to function. Because of this, meat dishes prepared in slow cookers don't turn out to be dry; rather, they are cooked for a longer period of time to keep their juicy and tender texture. A lot of recipes that use venison call for slow cookers. This is because deer meat, if not properly prepared, may have a flavor that is somewhat gamey. This has several causes, one of which is listed below.

Using slow cookers to give less expensive pieces of meat the same tender texture as more expensive cuts of meat can ultimately save you money if you cook for people who prefer more expensive cuts of meat. This is so that meat can simmer for a longer period of time at a lower temperature in slow cookers. Slow cookers make it simple to accomplish this goal when used with less expensive beef cuts.

4. Save money by using a slow cooker.

You can typically anticipate a significant decrease in the amount of money you spend on your monthly power bills if you start using your slow cooker more frequently than your oven. This is so that they cook food more slowly than traditional ovens, which use a higher temperature setting. Generally speaking, slow cookers use less electricity than other types of cookers, and given that they can cook more food at once, they are also more economical in the long run.

5. eat healthier.

If you frequently use kitchen appliances like stoves, ovens, and frying pans, you will eventually grow accustomed to the intense heat they produce. On the other hand, the nutrients in the food you eat are most likely being destroyed by the high temperatures. Meals that would otherwise be nutritious can become dishes with less nutrition when exposed to this kind of heat. Additionally, if used for a prolonged period of time, this type of heat has the potential to result in the release of potentially toxic chemical compounds that could be seriously harmful to your health.

The likelihood that the nutrients contained within the components will be retained increases and the likelihood that harmful substances will be produced decreases when food is cooked for an extended period of time at low temperatures.

6. Slow cookers can be cleaned with little effort.

Slow cookers are far easier to clean and maintain than any of the aforementioned options because food does not frequently stick to the bottom of them in the same way that it does in ovens and frying pans. A single slow cooker can be cleaned much more quickly and easily than a large collection of pots and pans.

7. Flexible Settings for Perfect Slow Cooker Results

Slow cookers no longer come in a single size that can accommodate everyone's needs; those days are long gone. Nowadays, the vast majority of slow cookers have a variety of settings and a respectable amount of space so that users can customize their cooking experience. It is still simple to use if you want your slow cooker to perform a more "basic" task, but if you want one with all the bells and whistles, you won't have any trouble finding that either.

8. Serve straight from the slow cooker

It usually takes some time for the food in a slow cooker to completely cool down, so anyone who wants seconds will find that their meal is still warm and ready to eat even after some time has passed. A 'keep warm' feature that allows the meal to be kept warm and ready to serve long after the cooking time has passed is included in the vast majority of slow cookers, which is better.

CHAPTER 3:
REASONS FOR USING CROCKPOT

"When meat is cooked at a low temperature for an extended length of time, the collagen and connective tissues have the chance to degrade, which makes the flesh softer. This occurs when the meat is cooked at a low temperature. It is possible to transform cheap cuts of meat into delicate, tasty morsels that fall apart in your mouth by cooking them at a low temperature for a lengthy period of time. This brings out the full flavor of the meals that are cooked in this manner.

If you want to purchase meat but keep your expenses down, one piece of guidance I can provide you is to do it online, which is another piece of information I can give you. The price of meat that is sold on the main street is far higher than the price that can be found at a variety of online butcher shops that give delivery the following day at a significantly reduced cost."

- **Save energy.**

"When compared to the energy consumption of an electric oven, the amount of power used by a slow cooker is far smaller. During each hour that it is operational, the typical home oven uses up around 4,000 watts of power. On the other hand, slow cookers need just 300 watts of electricity to function properly. On the other hand, if I have to cook my beef for an unspecified period of time, I don't see how this could possibly be more cost-effective. Wrong.

Let's say you had a piece of beef brisket that, in order to get the same results as roasting it in an oven for two hours, it would need to be cooked in a slow cooker for six hours. The slow cooker would still need a total of 1,800 watts of electricity, even if the cooking period would be far longer. To power the oven, 8000 watts are going to be required. Using a slow cooker rather than an oven is better for the environment and more cost effective given that the price of electricity is directly related to the amount of time it is on.

- **The cooking of the dishes is a very straightforward process.**

Slow cookers make it possible for anybody to become a skilled chef since almost all of the ingredients that are needed by the recipes are put all at once in the slow cooker. You may have to give them a quick stir just the once in order to ensure that they are evenly coated with the liquid and the spices, but other than that, there is nothing more that has to be done. If you just put the lid on the pot and walk away, you can keep all of the flavor and moisture within without doing anything more.

Only a handful of the recipes ask for stirring the food at varying intervals while it is being cooked. For almost all of the recipes that call for a slow cooker, it is absolutely OK to forget about the device for extended periods of time at a time without any negative consequences. In point of fact, the great majority of recipes stipulate that the lid must be left on the pot during the whole of the designated cooking time before it may be removed.

Do you like the flavor of a good curry? Take a look at these ideas for slow cooker curries that may be cooked in a variety of different ways.

- **An Abundance of Slow Cooker Cookbooks for Every Taste**

Since these portable cooking appliances have been in use since the middle of the 20th century, there is a plethora of literature devoted to their use that can be found on Amazon, in thrift shops, and on the shelves of libraries. Because of the recent surge in popularity of slow cookers, you will never run out of ideas for dishes to prepare, and there are specialized recipe books that are dedicated to slow cooking that cater to all different kinds of diets.

Having a slow cooker, particularly one of the larger versions, makes it much easier and quicker to prepare meals than doing so without one. The vast majority of recipes produce anywhere from six to eight servings, which guarantees that you will have sufficient food to consume over the course of a number of days.

You could create three or four different dishes in your slow cooker on Sunday and have enough food for the whole week, sparing you the stress of having to spend time in the kitchen each night trying to prepare meals. If you do this, you will have enough food for the whole week.

- **There is no danger involved in making use of them in any way.**

Is there any danger associated with using a slow cooker? Yes! They are designed to function without human supervision. Their maximum wattage is 300, which is the same as turning on three light bulbs that each needs 100 watts of electricity to operate.

If you are using an old banger with a frayed cord or indulging in any type of careless home electrical work, then it is not safe to use these cookers while you are gone or while you are asleep. However, it is safe to use these cookers while you are awake. It is quite uncommon that you will unintentionally ruin your meal by cooking it too long. There is a decreased chance of the food excessively drying out and catching fire as a consequence of the tight covers that are put on the cookers. This is something that is always a worry when cooking using an oven or stove.

- **The meal is wonderful in every possible manner.**

The scent of hearty soups and stews that have been gently simmering all day in the kitchen is one of the most comforting things to come home to after a hard day of work during the winter.

The dish is prepared by cooking it at a lower temperature for a much longer period of time, which helps to maintain the dish's essence. The meat in dishes that are made in a single pot nearly always comes out very soft, and these dishes blend a range of flavors in exciting and novel ways. Follow the link for forty meals that can be cooked right now in a slow cooker that will make your mouth wet.

- **Preparing meals that are healthier for you is not a tough task at all.**

The vitamins that are already present in food have a better chance of remaining when it is cooked at a low temperature for a prolonged period of time. Another way to boost the amount of nutrients a dish offers is to increase the amount of sauce or gravy it was cooked in before adding it to the finished dish.

Slow cookers are a fantastic alternative for you to consider, even if you have particular food preferences. A slow cooker can be used to cook a large quantity of vegetables in a variety of ways with ease. The savory flavor of the meat permeates the vegetables because the meat and vegetables are cooked at the same time, giving them a deliciously savory flavor.

If the idea of eating carrots that have been boiled turns you off, you can add carrots to your favorite stew and cook them in a slow cooker to change the flavor. The stew will taste more earthy as a result.

CHAPTER 4:
THE DOWNSIDES OF EMPLOYING THE USE OF A SLOW COOKER

"It's conceivable that you'll come to the conclusion that a slow cooker is an important small appliance to have in your kitchen; nevertheless, you shouldn't make that decision until you've completed reading through the material included in this section first.

- **A slow cooker is not a method that is considered to be efficient**

Since it takes a while to prepare anything, a slow cooker is not the best kitchen appliance to use when you need to prepare something quickly. You cannot cook quick meals if your hunger cannot wait that long because most slow cooker recipes require a minimum of three to four hours to prepare.

- **Not Suitable for Every Dish**

When a meal has several different components or contains ingredients that must be browned before cooking, it can be difficult to prepare it in a slow cooker.

As a result, the slow cooker can only be used to prepare specific kinds of meals, namely those that don't require adding a lot of ingredients at once. However, a slow cooker that can also be used as an instant cooker will have a sauté function that you can use to brown the food before adding it to the slow cooker to finish cooking.

Do you enjoy ham? Learn the best slow cooker methods for cooking pork to get the best results.

- **Slow Cooker Accuracy**

Given how hands-off using a slow cooker is, any mistakes that may be made during meal preparation cannot be easily fixed. You simply have no choice but to consume the food that you have laboriously prepared when using a slow cooker.

You will almost always need to make preparations in advance because the majority of meals may take three to twelve hours to prepare.

Read the article I wrote on how to use your slow cooker properly and avoid any mistakes to learn how to avoid disasters in the kitchen.

- **The influence that condensation has on the general quality of food**

You must make sure that you are ready to eat food that has been cooked in a small amount of water because condensation forms inside slow cookers.

This explains why a dinner may become a little soupy even when making soup wasn't the intended goal because the closed lid traps the steam, which later condenses into water. It's possible that the dish will end up tasting more like soup than it was intended to because the water dilutes the flavors and aromas.

Reduce the amount of liquid specified in the recipe by about a quarter to a half cup to avoid this from happening.

- **Some Flavors Have the Capacity to Dominantly Perform Among Others**

Strong flavors, especially those that have been cooked for a long time, can be overwhelmed by strong spices like cinnamon and thyme. This is especially valid if the food is hot when served.

It is strongly advised to use slightly fewer fresh spices than necessary or to add them toward the end of your cooking time when preparing meals in a slow cooker. Alternately, you could use a little less dried spice than is necessary. Additionally, it is strongly advised that you use a little less dried spice than is necessary. The recommendation is replaced by this.

CHAPTER 2
BREAKFAST

BREAKFAST CASSEROLE

Ingredients

- "8 eggs of medium size
- 200 grams of bacon, chopped into small pieces.
- 300 grams of sausage, crumbled, 200 grams of mushrooms, sliced
- 200 grams of cheddar cheese, and 500 milliliters of milk.
- Cubed bread from four slices and one teaspoon of salt
- Black pepper, 2 g
- Thyme, dried, in 2 g
- Dried parsley, 2 g"

Method

- ➤ "In a frying pan, cook the bacon over medium heat until it reaches the desired crispiness. Remove the bacon from the pan and set it aside in a different location. Drain the excess fat, leaving about a tablespoon in the pan.
- ➤ The sausage should be added to the pan and cooked until browned. Remove the sausage from the pan and store it somewhere else.
- ➤ In the same skillet, cook the chopped onion, green bell pepper, and sliced mushrooms until the onion and pepper are softened and the mushrooms are starting to turn light brown. After removing the pan from the heat, set it aside.
- ➤ In a sizable bowl, combine the eggs, milk, salt, black pepper, dried thyme, and dried parsley and whisk until well combined.
- ➤ Your slow cooker's interior should be greased with cooking spray or butter.
- ➤ Place half of the cubed bread, half of the cooked bacon and sausage, half of the sautéed vegetables, and half of the grated cheddar cheese in the bottom of the slow cooker. Utilizing the remaining parts, continue putting the layers together.
- ➤ In order to evenly distribute it, pour the egg mixture over the stacked ingredients in the slow cooker.
- ➤ For four to six hours, or until the eggs are the desired consistency and the casserole is thoroughly cooked, cook the casserole on low heat with the lid on the Crockpot.
- ➤ Remove the casserole's cover after the food has finished cooking and let it cool for a while before serving.
- ➤ The dish should be prepared in individual portions and served hot. If desired, you can add a garnish of additional herbs, like parsley, to the dish."

Ingredients:

- "500 grams of pork sausage
- 4 tablespoons of unsalted butter
- 4 tablespoons of plain flour
- 500 milliliters of milk
- 1/2 teaspoon of salt
- 1/4 teaspoon of black pepper
- 8 biscuits, homemade or store-bought, cut into quarters"

Method:

- "Prepare your oven by preheating it to 180 degrees Celsius (350 degrees Fahrenheit).
- Cook the pork sausage over medium heat in a frying pan until it is browned all the way through and is cooked through. Take the pan from the heat, and put it aside.
- Butter will need to be melted in a pot over medium heat. After stirring in the flour, continuing to boil the mixture for an additional one to two minutes should produce a thick paste.
- Pour the milk in a slow stream while whisking in the salt and black pepper until the mixture is smooth. Cook the mixture while stirring it constantly until it reaches a simmer and reaches the desired thickness.
- Take the skillet off the heat and toss in the pork sausage that has already been cooked.
- Put the biscuit quarters onto a baking dish that has been buttered. The biscuits should be well covered with the sausage gravy mixture once it has been poured over them.
- Bake the biscuits in an oven that has been prepared to 350 degrees for 25 to 30 minutes, or until they have a golden brown color all the way through.
- Serve piping hot as a mouthwatering casserole with sausage and gravy."

Ingredients:

- "1 loaf of white bread, preferably a day or two old, sliced
- 6 large eggs
- 500 milliliters of milk
- 100 grams of granulated sugar
- 1 tablespoon of vanilla extract
- 1/2 teaspoon of ground cinnamon
- A pinch of salt
- Butter, for greasing the slow cooker
- Maple syrup, for serving"

Method:

- ➢ "Butter should be used to coat the inside of your slow cooker.
- ➢ Place the sliced white bread in the slow cooker in a layered fashion after it has been buttered.
- ➢ In a dish, thoroughly mix the egg whites, whole milk, granulated sugar, vanilla essence, powdered cinnamon, and salt by whisking the ingredients together.
- ➢ To ensure that every piece of bread is wet, equally distribute the egg mixture over the bread pieces that are contained inside the slow cooker.
- ➢ Turn the heat down to low, cover the slow cooker and simmer the bread pudding for four to six hours, or until it has reached the desired consistency and is fully cooked.
- ➢ Warm the custard made with bread and butter and sprinkles it with maple syrup before serving".

SLOW COOKER EGG BREAKFAST CASSEROLE:

Ingredients:

- "12 large eggs
- 200 milliliters of milk
- 1 red bell pepper, diced
- 1 green bell pepper, diced
- 1 small onion, diced
- 200 grams of mushrooms, sliced
- 200 grams of cooked ham, diced
- 200 grams of cheddar cheese, grated
- 1 teaspoon of salt
- 1/2 teaspoon of black pepper"

Method:

- "A large bowl should be used to whisk the eggs, milk, salt, and black pepper until everything is thoroughly combined.
- Your slow cooker's interior should be coated with butter or nonstick cooking spray.
- Distribute the cooked ham, diced onion, sliced mushrooms, bell peppers, and cheddar cheese evenly in a slow cooker that has been greased.
- Make sure everything is thoroughly mixed before adding the egg mixture to the ingredients that are already in the slow cooker.
- For four to six hours, or until the eggs have set and the dish is thoroughly cooked, cook the casserole in the slow cooker with the eggs covered.
- Serve hot as a delicious slow-cooked egg breakfast casserole ".

Ingredients:

- "500 grams of frozen tater tots
- 200 grams of cooked bacon, crumbled
- 1 small onion, diced
- 1 red bell pepper, diced
- 200 grams of cheddar cheese, grated
- 8 large eggs
- 250 milliliters of milk
- 1 teaspoon of salt
- 1/2 teaspoon of black pepper"

Method:

- "Set your oven to 180 degrees Celsius to get ready (350 degrees Fahrenheit).
- Cooking spray or butter the inside of a baking dish, then set it aside.
- In the buttered baking dish, spread out the frozen tater tots in a single layer.
- Sprinkle the shredded cheddar cheese, chopped red bell pepper, chopped onion, and crumbled bacon over the tater tots.
- In a different bowl, whisk together the eggs, milk, salt, and black pepper until thoroughly combined.
- Make sure everything is evenly covered when you pour the egg mixture over the ingredients that have been placed in the baking dish.
- Bake for 45 to 50 minutes, or until the eggs have set and the casserole is the desired color, in a preheated oven.
- Make sure the casserole has had time to cool down before serving ".

Ingredients:

- 1 loaf of French bread, preferably a day or two old, sliced
- 6 large eggs
- 500 milliliters of milk
- 100 grams of granulated sugar
- 1 tablespoon of vanilla extract
- 1/2 teaspoon of ground cinnamon
- A pinch of salt
- 200 grams of blueberries (fresh or frozen)
- Icing sugar, for dusting

Method:

- Butter should be used to grease the inside of a slow cooker or Crockpot.
- Place the sliced French bread in the slow cooker in a layered fashion after it has been buttered.
- In a dish, thoroughly mix the egg whites, whole milk, granulated sugar, vanilla essence, powdered cinnamon, and salt by whisking the ingredients together.
- To ensure that every piece of bread gets drenched, pour the egg mixture over the bread pieces that are already in the slow cooker.
- Blueberries should be distributed equally over the top of the bread and egg mixture.
- Cook the French toast on low heat with the lid on the slow cooker for four to six hours, or until it is set and cooked all the way through.
- Immediately before to serving, dust with icing sugar.

Ingredients:

- 8 large eggs
- 500 milliliters of milk
- 8 slices of bread, cubed
- 200 grams of cooked bacon, crumbled
- 1 small onion, diced
- 200 grams of cheddar cheese, grated
- 1 teaspoon of salt
- 1/2 teaspoon of black pepper

Method:

- ➢ Prepare your oven by preheating it to 180 degrees Celsius (350 degrees Fahrenheit).
- ➢ Butter or coat the inside of a baking dish with cooking spray, then set aside.
- ➢ Whisk the eggs, milk, salt, and black pepper together in a large bowl using a whisk until everything is well incorporated.
- ➢ Place the cubed bread in the baking dish that has been buttered.
- ➢ On top of the toast, sprinkle some crumbled bacon, some chopped onion, and some shredded cheddar cheese.
- ➢ Pour the egg mixture over the stacked ingredients in the baking dish in a uniform and consistent manner to ensure that everything gets well covered.
- ➢ To ensure that the bread is well saturated in the egg mixture, give it a little pressing.
- ➢ Bake in an oven that has been warmed for 40 to 45 minutes or until the eggs have solidified and the casserole has reached the desired color.
- ➢ Before serving, make sure the casserole has had some time to cool down.

BACON AND BISCUIT SLOW COOKER CASSEROLE:

Ingredients:

- 250 grams of bacon, cooked and crumbled
- 8 refrigerated biscuits
- 6 large eggs
- 250 milliliters of milk
- 200 grams of cheddar cheese, grated
- 1/2 teaspoon of salt
- 1/4 teaspoon of black pepper

Method:

- ➤ Butter or cooking spray should be used to grease the inside of the slow cooker.
- ➤ Cut each of the biscuits that were stored in the refrigerator into quarters.
- ➤ In a bowl, thoroughly incorporate the eggs, milk, salt, and black pepper by whisking all of the ingredients together.
- ➤ Put one half of the biscuit quarters in the bottom of the slow cooker and then coat them with butter.
- ➤ On top of the biscuits, sprinkle one-half of the crumbled bacon and the cheddar cheese that has been granted.
- ➤ Over the stacked ingredients, pour half of the egg mixture that has been mixed together.
- ➤ Repeat the layering process with the remaining biscuit quarters, bacon, cheese, and egg mixture until all of the ingredients have been used.
- ➤ Cover the slow cooker and place it on low heat for six to eight hours or on high heat for three to four hours, and cook it until the eggs have set and the casserole is completely cooked through.
- ➤ Before serving, make sure the casserole has had some time to cool down.

Ingredients:

- 1 can of refrigerated cinnamon rolls
- 4 large eggs
- 250 milliliters of milk
- 100 grams of granulated sugar
- 1 teaspoon of vanilla extract
- 1/2 teaspoon of ground cinnamon
- Cream cheese icing (included with the cinnamon rolls)

Method:

- Butter or coat the inside of a baking dish with cooking spray, then set aside.
- Cut the cinnamon buns that were stored in the refrigerator into bite-sized pieces.
- Place the cinnamon roll pieces in the baking dish in a uniform layer. The dish should have been buttered.
- In a bowl, thoroughly incorporate the ground cinnamon, granulated sugar, vanilla extract, and eggs by whisking all of the ingredients together with a whisk.
- Pour the egg mixture over the cinnamon roll pieces in a uniform layer and make sure that they are well covered.
- Bake the cinnamon rolls in an oven that has been preheated to the temperature specified on the bag of cinnamon rolls.
- After it has been cooked, the casserole should have the cream cheese frosting drizzled over the top of it.

PUMPKIN FRENCH TOAST CASSEROLE:

Ingredients:

- 1 loaf of French bread, preferably a day or two old, sliced
- 6 large eggs
- 500 milliliters of milk
- 200 grams of pumpkin puree
- 100 grams of granulated sugar
- 1 tablespoon of vanilla extract
- 1 teaspoon of ground cinnamon
- 1/2 teaspoon of ground nutmeg
- A pinch of salt
- Maple syrup, for serving

Method:

- Butter or coat the inside of a baking dish with cooking spray, then set aside.
- Place the sliced French bread in the baking dish that has been buttered in a layered fashion.
- Eggs, milk, pumpkin puree, granulated sugar, vanilla essence, powdered cinnamon, ground nutmeg, and salt are mixed together in a bowl using a whisk until the ingredients are well incorporated.
- To ensure that every piece of bread gets drenched, pour the egg mixture over the bread pieces that are already in the baking dish.
- In order to give the bread time to soak up the pumpkin mixture, cover the baking dish, and place it in the refrigerator for at least 6 hours, preferably overnight.
- Prepare your oven by preheating it to 180 degrees Celsius (350 degrees Fahrenheit).
- Take the baking dish out of the refrigerator and let it to remain at room temperature for approximately a quarter of an hour.
- Bake the French toast in an oven that has been prepared for 40 to 45 minutes, or until it has reached the desired consistency and is completely cooked through.
- Offer the Pumpkin for Serving

Ingredients:

- 1 loaf of French bread, preferably a day or two old, sliced
- 6 large eggs
- 500 milliliters of milk
- 100 grams of granulated sugar
- 1 tablespoon of vanilla extract
- 100 grams of raspberries
- 100 grams of chocolate chips
- Icing sugar, for dusting

Method:

- Butter or coat the inside of a baking dish with cooking spray, then set aside.
- Place the sliced French bread in the baking dish that has been buttered in a layered fashion.
- Eggs, milk, granulated sugar, and vanilla essence are mixed together in a bowl using a whisk until they are well incorporated.
- To ensure that every piece of bread gets drenched, pour the egg mixture over the bread pieces that are already in the baking dish.
- Place the chocolate chips and raspberries in a random pattern on top of the bread and egg mixture.
- In order to give the bread time to soak in the mixture, cover the baking dish, and place it in the refrigerator for at least 6 hours, preferably overnight.
- Prepare your oven by preheating it to 180 degrees Celsius (350 degrees Fahrenheit).
- Take the baking dish out of the refrigerator and let it to remain at room temperature for approximately a quarter of an hour.
- Bake the French toast in an oven that has been prepared for 40 to 45 minutes, or until it has reached the desired consistency and is completely cooked through.
- Immediately before to serving, dust with icing sugar.

CHAPTER 3
APPETIZERS

SOUTHWESTERN STUFFED BELL PEPPERS:

Ingredients:

- 4 any-color bell peppers, halved, with seeds removed
- 200 grams of cooked, shredded chicken
- 1 can of rinsed and drained black beans
- cup of rice, cooked
- diced small onion
- diced red bell pepper.
- one tomato diced in a can
- teaspoon of cumin powder
- Chili powder, half a teaspoon
- 100 grams of grated cheddar cheese with a dash of black pepper and salt to taste
- for garnish: fresh cilantro

Method:

- ➤ To get ready, preheat your oven to 180 degrees Celsius (350 degrees Fahrenheit).
- ➤ The bell pepper halves should be placed in an oiled oven-safe dish.
- ➤ Cooked chicken, cooked black beans, cooked rice, diced bell peppers, diced tomatoes, ground cumin, chili powder, salt, and black pepper should all be combined in a large bowl. Combine entirely.
- ➤ Once you've filled each side of the bell pepper to the brim with the mixture, gently press it down.
- ➤ The stuffed peppers would benefit from having some cheddar cheese sprinkled on top.
- ➤ After lining the baking dish with aluminum foil and preheating the oven to 350 degrees Fahrenheit, put it in. Bake the dish for 25 to 30 minutes, or until the peppers are tender to the fork and the cheese is melted and bubbling.
- ➤ Remove from the oven, then sprinkle some fresh cilantro on each plate before serving.

SAUTÉED PEAS AND CARROTS IN HONEY BUTTER:

Ingredients:

- 200 grams of peas, frozen
- 300 grams of sliced carrots with 30 grams of butter
- Honey, 15 grams
- To taste, add salt and black pepper.

Method:

- ➤ Melt the butter in a sizable pan over medium heat.
- ➤ The carrots should be added to the pan and cooked for 3 to 4 minutes while being stirred occasionally.
- ➤ When the vegetables are tender, add the frozen peas to the pan and cook for an additional 3 to 4 minutes.
- ➤ To evenly coat the vegetables, drizzle the honey over them and stir.
- ➤ To taste, add salt and black pepper to the food.
- ➤ Cook the vegetables for a further 1-2 minutes, or until they are thoroughly covered in the honey butter mixture.
- ➤ Serve as a delicious side dish after being taken off the heat.

Ingredients:

- Peeled, cored, and chopped four apples
- Water, 30 grams
- Sugar, 30 grams
- Lemon juice, 1 teaspoon
- Various fruits for the compote, like berries or peach slices
- Yogurt or whipped cream for serving.

Method:

- Apples that have been chopped, water, sugar, and lemon juice are all combined in a pan. Stir to combine.
- After cooking the apples on a heat that is just a little bit above medium while stirring them occasionally, they ought to be soft and supple.
- To make applesauce, mash the cooked apples with a potato masher or a fork until they reach the desired consistency.
- The compote will be created by cooking the various fruits in a separate pan over low heat until they begin to soften and release their juices.
- Applesauce and fruit compote can be served together either warm or cold, depending on your preference.
- Before serving, you can add yogurt or whipped cream to the dish as desired.

VEGETABLE FRITTATA:

Ingredients:

- six giant eggs
- Milk, 100 milliliters
- one diced small onion, one diced red bell pepper, and one diced zucchini
- 100 grams of half-sized cherry tomatoes.
- Cheddar cheese, grated, weighing 50 grams.
- Olive oil, 1 tablespoon
- To taste, add salt and pepper.
- for garnish: fresh parsley

Method

- Set up the grill for medium-high heat cooking.
- Use a whisk to combine eggs, milk, salt, and black pepper in a bowl.
- In a pan that can be put in the oven, olive oil needs to be heated over medium heat.
- Add the diced red pepper, diced zucchini, and chopped onion to a pan over medium heat. Until the vegetables are the desired tenderness, sauté them for about 5 to 6 minutes.
- The sautéed vegetables should be covered with the egg mixture after it has been added to the pan.
- Over the egg mixture, arrange the tomato halves in a pretty pattern.
- Over the frittata's top, evenly distribute the shredded cheddar cheese.
- Cover the skillet with the lid after placing it on the preheated grill.
- The frittata should be cooked on the grill for ten to twelve minutes, or until the desired doneness is reached and the cheese has melted and bubbled.
- Take it off the grill and give it some time to cool.
- Before serving, garnish with fresh parsley.

Ingredients:

- 1 kg of boneless pork shoulder
- Juiced limes, two
- 2 minced chipotle peppers in adobo sauce
- 4 minced garlic cloves
- 2 teaspoons of cumin powder
- dried oregano, two teaspoons
- smoked paprika, 1 teaspoon
- a pinch of salt
- Black pepper, half a teaspoon
- twelve tiny corn tortillas
- frying with vegetable oil
- lettuce shredded for serving
- for serving, chopped tomatoes
- Avocado slices for serving
- for garnish: fresh cilantro

Method:

➢ Mix lime juice, minced chipotle peppers, minced garlic, ground cumin, dried oregano, smoked paprika, salt, and black pepper in a bowl to make a marinade.

➢ The marinade should be poured over the pork shoulder and put in a large bag that can be sealed. The bag should be kept in the fridge overnight or for at least four hours with the seal intact.

➢ Set your oven to 150 degrees Celsius to get ready (300 degrees Fahrenheit).

➢ Put the pork shoulder in a roasting pan after removing it from the marinade. Pork shoulder is roasted. The excess marinade should be discarded.

➢ Place the dish in a preheated oven after wrapping it in aluminum foil. The pig should be roast for four to five hours, or until it is easily shreddable.

➢ After removing the pork from the oven, give it some time to cool. Shred the meat into small pieces using two forks.

➢ Over medium heat, warm vegetable oil in a large pan. Small batches of the corn tortillas should be fried one at a time until they are golden and crispy. Onto some paper towels, pour the water.

➢ Start by putting a tablespoon of the pulled pork on each cooked tortilla before assembling the tostadas. Add some chopped tomatoes, avocado slices, lettuce that has been shredded, and fresh cilantro to finish.

Ingredients:

- 1 kg of boneless pork shoulder
- Olive oil, 2 tablespoons
- 1 thinly sliced onion, 4 minced garlic cloves
- Crushed tomatoes in one can
- Tomato paste, 2 tablespoons
- Balsamic vinegar, two tablespoons
- 1 teaspoon dried basil
- dried oregano, 1 tablespoon
- Sugar, 1 teaspoon
- To taste, add salt and black pepper.
- 4 bread rolls or ciabatta rolls
- for serving, sliced mozzarella cheese
- For garnish, use fresh basil leaves.

Method:

- ➤ Olive oil is heated over medium heat in a big pan to make the sauce. Add sliced onions and minced garlic to the dish. The onion should be cooked until it turns translucent, and the garlic should be cooked until it begins to smell good.
- ➤ Crushed tomatoes, tomato paste, balsamic vinegar, sugar, black pepper, dried basil, and dried oregano should all be combined in a skillet. Stir everything thoroughly.
- ➤ Before continuing, place the pork shoulder in the pan and make sure it is completely covered in tomato sauce.
- ➤ Reduce the heat to a low setting and cook the pork, covered, for an additional four to five hours, or until it is tender enough to shred.
- ➤ Remove the pork from the pan and give it a moment to cool. Shred the meat into small pieces using two forks.
- ➤ Set up the grill for medium-high heat cooking.
- ➤ Cut each of the ciabatta buns or bread rolls in half. Each of the rolls' bottom halves should have some of the shredded pork attached to it. Cut mozzarella cheese ought to be sprinkled on top.

CHAPTER 4
LUNCH RECIPES

BUTTERNUT SQUASH AND VEGETABLE CHILI:

Ingredients:

- 1 butternut squash, diced after being peeled and seeded
- Olive oil, two tablespoons
- 1 diced onion, 2 minced garlic cloves
- 1 carrot, diced; 1 red bell pepper, diced; 1 green bell pepper, diced
- 1 can (400 grams) shredded tomatoes
- 1 can (400 grams) rinsed and drained kidney beans
- Vegetable stock, 500 milliliters
- 10 grams of chili powder
- 1 teaspoon of cumin, ground
- a half-teaspoon of smoked paprika
- To taste, add salt and black pepper.
- coriander leaves, fresh

Method:

- To prepare the sauce, warm the olive oil in a large pot over medium heat.
- The diced onion and garlic should now be in a saucepan. Cooking the onion until it is tender is recommended.
- The saucepan should be filled with sliced carrots, red bell peppers, and butternut squash. The vegetables should be cooked for a few more minutes, or until you reach the desired level of tenderness.
- Chop the tomatoes and add them to the mixture along with the kidney beans, cumin powder, smoked paprika, chili powder, salt, and black pepper. Stir everything together until it is distributed evenly.
- When the butternut squash is tender, the mixture should be simmered for 30 minutes after reaching a boil.
- If necessary, adjust the seasoning.
- Serve the chili in bowls while it's still hot, garnished with freshly chopped coriander.

Ingredients

- 100 grams of ground beef
- a half-cup of breadcrumbs
- 1 egg, 2 minced garlic cloves
- 1/4 cup of parmesan cheese
- one tablespoon dried basil
- Oregano, dried, 1 teaspoon
- 0.5 teaspoons of salt
- Black pepper, 1/4 teaspoon
- 1 can of diced tomatoes and 4 cups of beef broth
- 1 cup of carrots, chopped.
- three cups of chopped celery, onions, and zucchini.
- Chopped bell peppers, 1 cup

Methods:

- ➢ Ground beef, breadcrumbs, Parmesan cheese, egg, garlic, basil, oregano, salt, and black pepper are all combined in a bowl. Mix thoroughly, then form into small meatballs.
- ➢ Put the meatballs in the slow cooker.
- ➢ To the Crock Pot, add beef broth, diced tomatoes, carrots, celery, onions, zucchini, and bell peppers.
- ➢ Cook covered for 6 to 8 hours on low heat or for 3 to 4 hours on high heat.
- ➢ If desired, top with fresh parsley or basil before serving.

PUMPKIN AND VEGETABLE WHITE CHILI:

Ingredients:

- Olive oil, two tablespoons
- 1 diced onion
- 2 minced garlic cloves
- One can (400 grams) of white beans, drained and rinsed; one red bell pepper, diced; one green bell pepper, diced; one carrot, diced.
- 250 grams of pumpkin, diced.
- Vegetable stock, 500 milliliters
- 1 teaspoon of cumin, ground
- Oregano, dried, 1 teaspoon
- 1/8 teaspoon coriander powder
- a half-teaspoon of chili flakes (optional)
- To taste, add salt and black pepper.
- for garnish: fresh parsley

Method:

➤ In a big pot, heat the olive oil over medium heat to make the sauce.
➤ The saucepan should now contain the minced garlic and diced onion. The onion should be cooked until it is soft.
➤ Bell peppers, carrots, white beans, pumpkin, diced pumpkin, ground cumin, dried oregano, ground coriander, chili flakes (if using), salt, and black pepper should all be combined in a sizable saucepan.
➤ Once the mixture has reached a boil, turn down the heat, cover, and simmer for about 30 minutes, or until the pumpkin is tender.
➤ Make seasoning adjustments if required.
➤ Serve the white chili at a high temperature and garnish with fresh parsley.

HARVEST VEGETABLE CHILI:

Ingredients:

- Olive oil, two tablespoons
- 1 diced onion
- 2 minced garlic cloves
- one carrot, one zucchini, one red bell pepper, one green bell pepper, and one diced green bell pepper.
- 400 grams of diced tomatoes in one can
- 1 can (400 grams) rinsed and drained kidney beans
- Vegetable stock, 500 milliliters
- 10 grams of chili powder
- 1 teaspoon of cumin, ground
- a half-teaspoon of smoked paprika
- To taste, add salt and black pepper.
- for garnish: fresh parsley

Method:

- Over medium heat, warm the olive oil in a large pot.
- To the pot, add the minced garlic and onion. Cook the onion until it begins to soften.
- Add the kidney beans, diced tomatoes, diced zucchini, diced carrots, diced bell peppers, ground cumin, smoked paprika, salt, and black pepper to the pot.
- The mixture should be heated until it boils, then it should be simmered for about 30 minutes, or until the vegetables are soft.
- If necessary, adjust the seasoning.
- Serve the chili made with seasonal vegetables hot and topped with fresh parsley.

Ingredients:

- 1 lb. of skinless, boneless chicken breasts
- 1 can of rinsed and drained black beans
- Green chilies and diced tomatoes in one can
- Frozen corn, 250 grams
- 250 g diced bell peppers and onions
- 2 minced garlic cloves
- 4 cups of chicken stock
- one tablespoon of chili powder
- 1/9 cup cumin
- Paprika, half a teaspoon
- pepper and salt as desired
- Avocado, cilantro, tortilla chips, shredded cheese, and

mETHOD:

- ➤ Chicken breasts should be put in the Crock Pot.
- ➤ To the Crock Pot, add the following ingredients: black beans, diced tomatoes, corn, onion, bell peppers, garlic, chicken broth, chili powder, cumin, paprika, salt, and pepper.
- ➤ Cook covered for 6 to 8 hours on low heat or for 3 to 4 hours on high heat.
- ➤ Utilizing two forks, remove the chicken breasts from the Crock Pot.
- ➤ Stir well when adding the shredded chicken back to the slow cooker.
- ➤ Serve hot and garnish with tortilla chips, cheese, avocado, and cilantro.

TEX-MEX SCALLOPED POTATO AND CARROT BAKE:

Ingredients:

- 700 grams of potatoes, thinly sliced and peeled
- 2 peeled and thinly sliced carrots
- 1 thinly sliced onion
- 2 minced garlic cloves
- 1 can (400 grams) shredded tomatoes
- 200 gram cheddar cheese, grated
- Vegetable stock, 200 milliliters
- 1 teaspoon of cumin, ground
- one tablespoon of chili powder
- To taste, add salt and black pepper.
- coriander leaves, fresh

Method:

➢ Set your oven to 180 degrees Celsius to get ready (350 degrees Fahrenheit).
➢ In a sizable baking dish, arrange the sliced potatoes, carrots, onions, and garlic in alternating layers.
➢ In a separate bowl, thoroughly mix the diced tomatoes, grated cheese, vegetable stock, ground cumin, chili powder, salt, and black pepper to make the salsa.
➢ To ensure that all of the vegetables are thoroughly covered, the tomato sauce should be carefully poured over the pile of vegetables in the baking dish.
➢ Bake in a preheated oven for 45 minutes with the baking dish covered with aluminum foil.
➢ Remove the aluminum foil and bake the vegetables for an additional 15 minutes, or until they are tender and the top is golden.
➢ Add freshly chopped coriander to each portion just before serving.

Ingredients:

- 500 grams of cooked and shredded boneless, skinless chicken breasts
- 250 grams of rice, cooked.
- 400 grams of rinsed and drained black beans
- diced red bell pepper.
- diced green bell pepper.
- diced small onion.
- teaspoon of cumin, ground
- one tablespoon of chili powder
- To taste, add salt and black pepper.
- coriander leaves, fresh
- sour cream, salsa, guacamole, or any other desired toppings

Method:

- In a large pan over medium heat, cook the diced bell peppers and onion until the vegetables are soft.
- Shred the chicken and add it to the pan once it has finished cooking. Combine all of the ingredients.
- Combine the black beans with the ground cumin, chili powder, salt, and black pepper. Cook the food until it is thoroughly heated.
- Divide the cooked rice among the serving utensils.
- The rice should be topped with the chicken and vegetable mixture.
- Serve with any desired toppings, such as salsa, guacamole, sour cream, and fresh coriander, as a garnish.

RASPBERRY CHIPOTLE CHICKEN TACOS:

Ingredients:

- 500 g chicken breasts, skinless and without any bones
- 200 g of raspberries, fresh
- 2 minced chipotle peppers in adobo sauce
- Olive oil, two tablespoons
- Honey, two tablespoons
- a teaspoon of lime juice
- To taste, add salt and black pepper.
- 8 miniature tortillas
- for garnish: fresh cilantro

Method:

- ➤ Set your oven to 180 degrees Celsius to get ready (350 degrees Fahrenheit).
- ➤ Use a food processor or blender to combine fresh raspberries, minced chipotle peppers, olive oil, honey, lime juice, salt, and black pepper. Mix thoroughly until lumps are gone.
- ➤ The raspberry chipotle mixture should be poured over the chicken breasts after they have been put in a baking dish. The chicken needs to be completely covered.
- ➤ The chicken should be cooked for 20 to 25 minutes, or until it reaches an internal temperature of 165 degrees Fahrenheit, in a preheated oven.
- ➤ Take the chicken out of the oven and give it a few minutes to cool. Shred the chicken into small pieces using two forks.
- ➤ The tortillas should be warmed according to the packaging's instructions.
- ➤ Each tortilla should be filled with chicken shredded.

SLOW-ROASTED CHICKEN AND VEGETABLES:

Ingredients:

- 1 chicken, whole (approximately 1.5 kg)
- 500 grams of quartered and peeled potatoes
- two carrots, peeled and chopped
- 1 quartered onion
- 4 minced garlic cloves
- Olive oil, two tablespoons
- 1 tablespoon dried herbs, all kinds
- To taste, add salt and black pepper.
- for garnish: fresh parsley

Method:

- ➤ Set your oven to 160 degrees Celsius to get ready (320 degrees Fahrenheit).
- ➤ Prepare the chicken for cooking by placing it in a roasting pan.
- ➤ Before adding them to the basin with the rest of the ingredients, combine the potatoes, carrots, onion, minced garlic, dried mixed herbs, black pepper, and salt in a bowl.
- ➤ After placing the vegetable mixture around the chicken in the roasting pan, add the chicken to the pan.
- ➤ For two to two and a half hours, or until the chicken is cooked through and the vegetables are soft, roast the chicken and vegetables in the preheated oven. Wrap foil around the roasting pan.
- ➤ Remove the foil from the chicken and vegetables during the final 30 minutes of cooking so they can brown.
- ➤ Put the chicken and vegetables in a dish for serving after everything has finished cooking.
- ➤ Garnish with some freshly chopped parsley before serving.

CHAPTER 5
POULTRY RECIPES

CREAMY CHICKEN AND VEGETABLE ALFREDO:

Ingredients:

- 500 grams of sliced, skinless, and boneless chicken breasts
- Olive oil tablespoon
- diced onion
- 2 minced garlic cloves
- one red pepper, diced, and one green pepper, diced.
- 200 milliliters of double cream and 200 grams of sliced mushrooms
- 100 grams of parmesan cheese, grated.
- To taste, add salt and black pepper.
- 250 grams of the pasta of your choice, cooked per the directions on the package, with fresh parsley for garnish.

Method:

➢ In a large pan, the olive oil should be heated to a medium temperature.

- A pan should be filled with onion diced and minced garlic. Cooking the onion until it is tender is recommended.
- Cook the chicken strips in the pan after adding them, turning them over once or twice, until all sides are browned and the chicken is no longer pink in the middle.
- Chicken should be taken out of the pan and saved for later.
- The same pan should also contain the sliced mushrooms and bell peppers, which should be chopped. After cooking, the vegetables ought to be fork-tender.
- Add the double cream and Parmesan cheese to the pan once the heat has been reduced to a low setting. While stirring, wait for the cheese to melt and the sauce to become creamy.
- To taste, you can add seasonings like salt and black pepper.
- When the chicken is done cooking, return it to the pan and stir it to distribute the creamy sauce evenly.
- You can serve fettuccine or any other cooked pasta you prefer on top of the rich, creamy chicken and vegetable Alfredo sauce.
- Before serving, garnish with some freshly chopped parsley.

Ingredients:

- 500 g chicken breasts, skinless and without any bones
- Olive oil, two tablespoons
- 2 minced garlic cloves
- 200 grams of cherry tomatoes, cut in half, 1 can, 1 onion, diced, 1 red bell pepper, diced, 1 yellow bell pepper, diced (400 grams) shredded tomatoes.
- 1 teaspoon each of dried basil and oregano
- To taste, add salt and black pepper.
- garnished with fresh basil.

Method:

- ➤ The olive oil should be heated to a medium temperature in a big pan.
- ➤ Sliced onion and minced garlic should be added to the pan. The onion should be cooked until it is soft.
- ➤ Place the chicken breasts in the skillet and cook them until they are cooked through and have a brown crust on both sides. Remove the chicken from the pan and reserve it for later.
- ➤ In the same skillet, combine the chopped bell peppers and the half-cut cherry tomatoes. The vegetables should be fork-tender after cooking.
- ➤ The chopped tomatoes, dried basil and dried oregano, some salt, and some black pepper should all be added to the pan. Mix by stirring.
- ➤ Re-add the cooked chicken to the pan, lower the heat to a simmer, and let the flavors mingle for a while.
- ➤ Before serving, reheat the Italian-style chicken and top it with fresh basil.

Ingredients:

- 500 grams of sliced, skinless, and boneless chicken breasts
- Olive oil, two tablespoons
- 1 diced onion
- 2 minced garlic cloves
- Double cream in 200 milliliters
- 200 ml of chicken stock
- Dijon mustard, two tablespoons
- 1 tablespoon of freshly chopped thyme
- To taste, add salt and black pepper.
- for garnish: fresh parsley

Method:

- In a large pan, bring the olive oil to a temperature of medium heat.
- Garlic that has been minced and diced onion should be added to a pan. The onion should be cooked until it is soft.
- Add the chicken strips to the pan and cook them until they are no longer pink in the middle and have browned on all sides.
- Remove the chicken from the pan and reserve it for later.
- Add the double cream, chicken stock, Dijon mustard, chopped fresh thyme, and your preferred amounts of salt, black pepper, and white pepper to the same pan. Mix by stirring.
- As the creamy sauce starts to slightly thicken, keep it simmering on low heat for a few minutes, stirring every so often.
- After the chicken has finished cooking, add it back to the pan and stir it until the creamy sauce is evenly distributed throughout.
- To fully warm the chicken, cook it for a further two to three minutes.
- While the chicken is still hot, top it with the creamy sauce and top with fresh parsley.

MANGO-GLAZED CHICKEN:

Ingredients:

- 500 g chicken breasts, skinless and without any bones
- 2 tablespoons of olive oil
- 4 tablespoons of mango chutney
- 1 teaspoon each of lime juice and honey
- 2 teaspoons of grated ginger
- To taste, add salt and black pepper.
- coriander leaves, fresh

Method:

- ➢ Heat your grill or barbeque to a setting between medium and high to get it ready.
- ➢ Mango chutney, soy sauce, lime juice, honey, ginger that has been grated, salt, and black pepper should all be combined in a bowl.
- ➢ The chicken breasts should be seasoned with salt and black pepper after being coated in olive oil.
- ➢ When the chicken is fully cooked, place it on the grill or barbecue and cook for six to eight minutes on each side.
- ➢ Apply the mango glaze to the chicken with a pastry brush during the last few minutes of cooking. While doing this, flip the chicken over to make sure all sides are coated.
- ➢ To allow the juices to redistribute, remove the chicken from the grill or barbecue and let it sit for a few minutes.
- ➢ Slice the chicken and top it with freshly chopped coriander just before serving.

Ingredients:

- 500 grams of cubed, skinless, and boneless chicken breasts
- 200 grams of sliced, smoked sausage with two tablespoons of vegetable oil
- 1 diced onion
- 2 celery stalks, diced, 1 green bell pepper,
- 3 minced garlic cloves
- 400 grams tomato dice in a can
- 500 ml container of chicken stock
- 1 bay leaf, 2
- one tablespoon of dried thyme
- smoked paprika, 1 teaspoon.
- a half-teaspoon of cayenne (adjust to taste)
- To taste, add salt and black pepper.
- served with cooked rice.
- Green onions, chopped, as a garnish

Method:

- ➢ The vegetable oil should be heated to a medium temperature in a big pot or Dutch oven.
- ➢ Stir the celery, diced green bell pepper, diced green bell pepper, minced garlic, and chopped onion together in the saucepan. Cook the vegetables for the desired amount of time.
- ➢ Place the sausage slices and chicken cubes in the saucepan. To combine, stir. The chicken should continue to cook until both sides are golden brown.
- ➢ Add the chicken stock, bay leaves, dried thyme, smoked paprika, cayenne pepper, salt, and black pepper along with the chopped tomatoes from the can.
- ➢ After bringing the mixture to a full boil, reduce the heat to a low setting. Cook the mixture over low heat for about an hour, or until the chicken is thoroughly cooked and tender.
- ➢ Remove the bay leaves from the saucepan and throw them away.
- ➢ The cooked rice should be topped with the chicken and sausage gumbo before serving.
- ➢ Add some finely chopped green onions to the top of each serving before serving.

CHAPTER 6
BEEF, PORK AND LAMB RECIPES

MARINATED BEEF SKEWERS WITH SPICY GINGER AND GARLIC:

Ingredients:

- 500 grams of cubed beef sirloin
- 2/fourths cup soy sauce
- Worcestershire sauce, two tablespoons
- Olive oil, two tablespoons
- 2 tablespoons of ginger, grated.
- 4 minced garlic cloves
- 1 teaspoon of the spicy flakes (adjust to taste)
- To taste, add salt and black pepper.
- Water-soaked wooden skewers

Method:

➢ The soy sauce, Worcestershire sauce, olive oil, minced garlic, grated ginger, chili flakes, salt, and black pepper should all be combined in a bowl.

- The meat cubes should be thoroughly coated in the marinade before being added to the dish. For best results, leave the bowl covered in the fridge for at least an hour or overnight.
- Heat your grill or barbeque to a setting between medium and high to get it ready.
- Put the soaked wooden skewers on which you will skewer the marinated beef cubes.
- When the meat is cooked to the desired level of doneness, place the skewers on the grill or barbecue and cook for about 4-5 minutes on each side.
- Before using the skewers again, remove them from the grill or barbecue and let them cool for a while.
- When served hot, the beef skewers that have been marinated in hot ginger and garlic make a delicious appetizer or main dish.

Ingredients:

- Roast beef weighing 1.5 kg
- Vegetable oil, two tablespoons
- 2 sliced onions
- 4 carrots, peeled and chopped.
- four celery stalks, chopped
- 4 minced garlic cloves
- a 500 ml container of beef stock
- a 250 ml bottle of red wine (optional)
- 1 bay leaf, 2
- a serving of Worcestershire sauce
- ¼ cup tomato paste
- ¼ cup dried thyme
- To taste, add salt and black pepper.

Method:

- Set your oven to 160 degrees Celsius to get ready (320 degrees Fahrenheit).
- In a sizable Dutch oven or other oven-safe pot, heat the vegetable oil to the proper temperature over medium heat.
- The beef chuck roast should be seasoned with salt and black pepper before being set aside. Sear the roast in the hot oil for a few minutes to brown it on both sides. Remove the roast from the oven, then set it somewhere else.
- In the same saucepan as the chicken, add the minced garlic, chopped carrots, celery, and onion slices. Cook the vegetables for the desired amount of time.
- Put the previously seared beef chuck roast back into the pan. Add the beef stock, red wine (if using), bay leaves, Worcestershire sauce, tomato paste, dried thyme, salt, and pepper to the dish. Mix by stirring.
- When the pot is warmed, place it in the oven while it is covered with its lid. The beef should be cooked for about three to four hours, or until it is tender and easy to shred.
- Allow the pot roast to rest for a few minutes after removing it from the oven before slicing or shredding it.
- The cooked vegetables and pan juices should be served alongside the classic pot roast.

Ingredients:

- 500 grams of cubed beef stew meat
- Vegetable oil, two tablespoons
- 1 diced onion
- 2 minced garlic cloves
- 1 diced red bell pepper
- 400 grams of diced tomatoes in one can
- Tomato paste, two tablespoons
- a 400 ml container of beef stock
- 1 can (400 grams) rinsed and drained kidney beans
- Chipotle paste, two teaspoons
- 2 teaspoons each of ground cumin and paprika
- Oregano, dried, 1 teaspoon
- To taste, add salt and black pepper.
- serving of sour cream
- coriander leaves, fresh

Method:

- ➢ The vegetable oil should be heated to a medium temperature in a big pot or Dutch oven.
- ➢ Place the minced garlic, diced red bell pepper, and chopped onion in the saucepan. Cook the vegetables for the desired amount of time.
- ➢ Remove the beef stew meat from the pot after browning it on both sides in the saucepan.
- ➢ Diced tomatoes, tomato paste, beef stock, kidney beans, chipotle paste, ground cumin, paprika, dried oregano, and a dash of salt and black pepper should all be added to the saucepan. To combine, stir.
- ➢ After bringing the mixture to a full boil, reduce the heat to a low setting. Place the saucepan on the stovetop with low heat and cover it. Spend about two hours simmering, or until the beef is tender and the flavors are well-balanced.
- ➢ Season the food as needed with additional salt and freshly ground black pepper.
- ➢ Serve the chipotle beef chili hot, topped with a dollop of sour cream, and garnished with fresh coriander.

Ingredients:

- 1.5 kilograms of roast pork
- Olive oil, two tablespoons
- 4 minced garlic cloves
- rosemary, dried, in two tablespoons
- ¼ cup dried thyme
- Paprika, 1 tablespoon
- Brown sugar, 1 tablespoon
- 1 salt shakerful
- Black pepper, half a teaspoon
- 250 milliliters of apple cider vinegar and 500 milliliters of chicken stock

Method:

- ➤ Set your oven to 150 degrees Celsius to get ready (300 degrees Fahrenheit).
- ➤ In a small bowl, mix the minced garlic, paprika, dried rosemary, dried thyme, brown sugar, salt, and black pepper to make a rub. Mix thoroughly. Place aside.
- ➤ The pork shoulder roast should be completely covered in olive oil and should have the oil rubbed into all of its surfaces.
- ➤ The pork will be thoroughly coated if the prepared rub is massaged onto it.
- ➤ A roasting pan or Dutch oven should be used to cook the pork shoulder roast.
- ➤ Pour the chicken stock and apple cider vinegar reduction into the pan but not directly on top of the pork.
- ➤ The roasting pan or Dutch oven should be covered with a lid or aluminum foil.
- ➤ Roast the pork for four to five hours at a low temperature in a preheated oven, or until the meat is tender and easily shreds with a fork.
- ➤ Turn the oven's temperature up to 220 degrees Celsius and remove the cover or foil (425 degrees Fahrenheit). Roast the pork for a further 15 to 20 minutes, or until the top is crisp and browned.
- ➤ After the pig has been slowly roasted, remove it from the oven, let it rest for about ten minutes, and then slice or shred it.
- ➤ The hot, slow-roasted pork is a fantastic main course that goes well with any side dishes you choose.

Ingredients:

- 1.5 kg roast beef (such as sirloin or rib eye)
- Olive oil, two tablespoons
- 2 tablespoons of coffee grounds
- Brown sugar 2 tablespoons
- 15 grams of paprika, cumin, garlic, and salt powder 1 teaspoon of black pepper, ground
- 1 salt shakerful

Method:

- ➢ Set your oven's temperature to 180 °C (350 °F).
- ➢ To make the spice rub, mix the ground coffee, brown sugar, paprika, cumin, black pepper, salt, garlic powder, and onion powder in a small bowl.
- ➢ Rub the olive oil all over the beef roast after patting it dry with paper towels.
- ➢ The beef roast should have the spice rub applied evenly and pressed into the meat.
- ➢ The seasoned beef roast should be placed on a roasting rack inside a roasting pan.
- ➢ Depending on the weight of the beef, roast it in the preheated oven for 25 minutes per pound, or until the internal temperature reaches the desired doneness. When using a meat thermometer, aim for an internal temperature of 55–60°C (130–140°F) for medium-rare.
- ➢ When the roast has reached the doneness you prefer, remove it from the oven and loosely tent it with foil. Before slicing, let it sit for about 15 minutes.
- ➢ Slice the roast beef with java spices thinly, against the grain.
- ➢ Serve the roast beef hot with your favorite side dishes as the centerpiece of a delectable meal.

CHAPTER 7
SEA FOOD, FISH RECIPES

SLOW COOKER COCONUT CURRY SHRIMP:

Ingredients:

- 500 grams of peeled and deveined shrimp
- 400 ml of coconut milk in a can
- 1 diced onion
- 2 minced garlic cloves
- Sliced red bell pepper, carrot, and two tablespoons of curry powder
- 5 g each of ground paprika, cumin, and turmeric
- To taste, add salt and black pepper.
- chopped fresh coriander for adornment
- served with cooked rice

Method:

- ➢ A slow cooker should be filled with coconut milk, minced garlic, minced onion, sliced red bell pepper, sliced carrot, curry powder, ground cumin, ground turmeric, and paprika. Give everything a good stir to combine.
- ➢ Move the prawns around in the slow cooker after you've added them to ensure that the curry sauce coats them all equally.
- ➢ To fully cook the prawns, reduce the heat to low, cover the slow cooker, and simmer it for two to three hours.
- ➢ The prawns in the coconut curry should be garnished with freshly chopped coriander after they have finished cooking.
- ➢ Prawns cooked in coconut curry can be served over hot, cooked rice for a flavorful and fragrant dinner.

CROCKPOT LEMON GARLIC BUTTER FISH:

Ingredients:

- 4 fillets of fish (such as cod or tilapia)
- 4 tablespoons of melted butter
- lemon juice from one
- 2 minced garlic cloves
- one tablespoon of dried thyme
- To taste, add salt and black pepper.
- chopped fresh parsley for a garnish

Method:

- ➤ The slow cooker should be filled with the fish fillets.
- ➤ Melted butter, lemon juice, chopped garlic, dried thyme, salt, and black pepper should be combined in a low-sided bowl.
- ➤ You can start cooking the fish after making sure the lemon-garlic-butter mixture is evenly applied to the fish fillets.
- ➤ When the fish is fully cooked and easily flakes apart when tested with a fork, cook it in the slow cooker for two to three hours on low heat with the lid on.
- ➤ Sprinkle some freshly chopped parsley over the fish that has been cooked in lemon garlic butter once it has finished cooking.
- ➤ Serve the fish while it is still hot for a meal that is flavorful and succulent.

Ingredients:

- 500 grams of cleaned and rinsed clams
- 2 bacon slices, 1 onion, 2 celery stalks, 2 potatoes, peeled, and diced
- 2 cups of vegetable or fish stock
- a cup of milk
- 50 ml of heavy cream
- 2 tablespoons of regular flour
- To taste, add salt and black pepper.
- chopped fresh parsley for a garnish.

Method:

- In a big pan over medium heat, cook the bacon cubes until crispy. Keep the bacon grease in the pan it was cooked in and add the bacon to the slow cooker.
- In the same pan, cook the chopped celery and onion over medium heat until the vegetables are tender. Put the bowl's contents in the slow cooker.
- Add the potatoes and your preferred stock to the slow cooker (fish or veggie). Depending on when they become soft, cook the potatoes, covered, for 6–8 hours on a low heat or 3–4 hours on a high heat.
- Use a whisk to thoroughly blend the milk, heavy cream, and all-purpose flour in a low-sided bowl. Transfer the mixture to the slow cooker once everything has been combined.
- When the clams are added to the slow cooker, cover it and cook it on high for another 30 minutes, or until the clams open.
- Add salt and freshly ground black pepper to taste when seasoning the clam chowder. Add some freshly chopped parsley to the dish just before serving.

CROCKPOT THAI COCONUT FISH CURRY:

Ingredients:

- 500 grams of white fish fillets, chopped
- 400 ml of coconut milk in a can
- Red curry paste, two tablespoons
- 10 ml of fish sauce
- Brown sugar, 1 tablespoon
- 1 sliced red bell pepper
- 1 sliced zucchini 1 sliced carrot
- chopped fresh coriander for adornment.
- wedges of lime for serving
- served with cooked rice.

Method:

- ➤ In a slow cooker, combine the coconut milk, brown sugar, fish sauce, and red curry paste. Stir everything together until it's all incorporated.
- ➤ In the slow cooker, combine the fish pieces with the red pepper, zucchini, and carrot that have been chopped. To evenly distribute the curry sauce, combine everything and stir.
- ➤ When the fish is fully cooked and the vegetables are soft, reduce the heat to low, cover the slow cooker, and let it simmer for two to three hours.
- ➤ Freshly chopped coriander ought to be added as a garnish to the Thai coconut fish curry once it has finished cooking. The lime wedges should be served with the cooked rice.

Ingredients:

- Scallops, 500 grams
- 4 tablespoons of melted butter 4 minced garlic cloves
- Juice from 1 lemon 2 tablespoons finely chopped fresh parsley
- To taste, add salt and black pepper.

Method:

- ➤ The scallops should be dried off with paper towels after being cleaned in ice-cold water.
- ➤ Melted butter, minced garlic, chopped parsley, lemon juice, salt, and black pepper should all be combined in a bowl with a low edge.
- ➤ Pour the garlic butter mixture over the scallops in the slow cooker and give them a quick stir to make sure they are all evenly coated.
- ➤ Cook the scallops in the slow cooker for one to two hours on low heat with the lid on, or until they are tender and cooked through.
- ➤ Scallops cooked in garlic butter in the slow cooker should be served hot as a delicious seafood dish.

CROCKPOT TERIYAKI SALMON:

Ingredients:

- 4 fillets of salmon
- a liter of soy sauce
- Honey, 60 ml
- Rice vinegar, two tablespoons
- Sesame oil, two tablespoons
- 2 minced garlic cloves
- 1 teaspoon of ginger, grated.
- Sesame seeds for decoration
- sliced spring onions for a garnish
- served with cooked rice.

Method:

- Soy sauce, honey, rice vinegar, sesame oil, minced garlic, and grated ginger should all be combined in a small bowl. Combine all of the ingredients.
- Pour the teriyaki sauce over the salmon fillets after placing them in the slow cooker, making sure to completely cover them.
- When the salmon is thoroughly cooked and easily flakes apart when tested with a fork, cook it in the slow cooker for two to three hours on low heat with the lid on.
- Top the cooked salmon teriyaki with sesame seeds and finely chopped spring onions.
- For a filling and delicious lunch, serve the salmon over hot, freshly made rice.

CHAPTER 8
SOUP

"CROCKPOT POTATO SOUP:

Ingredients:

- 500 grams of diced and peeled potatoes
- 1 diced onion, 2 minced garlic cloves
- 4 cups of chicken or vegetable stock
- 20 ml of double cream
- 0.5 g of butter
- To taste, add salt and black pepper.
- chopped fresh chives as a garnish.

Method:

➤ Add the cubed potatoes, onions, and minced garlic to the slow cooker along with the chicken or vegetable stock. Mix by stirring.

- ➤ Until the potatoes are the desired tenderness, cover the slow cooker and simmer on low heat for six to eight hours or on high heat for three to four hours.
- ➤ Use a hand blender or an immersion blender to partially blend the soup to make it creamier and thicker. A potato masher is an additional option.
- ➤ Stir in the double cream and butter after thoroughly combining. Seasonings like salt and black pepper can be added to taste.
- ➤ Put the lid on the slow cooker and simmer for an additional 30 minutes at low heat.
- ➤ The freshly chopped chives should be placed on top of the hot potato soup when it is served.

Ingredients:

- 500 grams of skinless, boneless chicken breasts
- 1 diced onion
- 2 minced garlic cloves
- 1 diced red bell pepper
- 400 grams tomato dice
- 400 grams of rinsed and drained black beans.
- 200 grams of drained sweet corn
- 10 grams of chili powder
- 1 teaspoon of cumin, ground
- 1 paprika teaspoon
- Oregano, dried, 1 teaspoon
- chicken stock, 4 cups
- To taste, add salt and black pepper.
- To serve with, tortilla chips
- chopped fresh coriander for adornment.
- wedges of lime for serving

Method:

- ➢ In the slow cooker, combine the chicken breasts, diced red bell pepper, diced tomatoes, diced onion, minced garlic, black beans, sweet corn, chili powder, cumin, paprika, dried oregano, and chicken stock. To combine, stir. Mix by stirring.
- ➢ Put the lid on top of the slow cooker and cook the chicken for six to eight hours on low heat or for three to four hours on high heat, depending on how soft you want it.
- ➢ ☐ Remove the chicken breasts from the slow cooker and shred them into small pieces using two forks. Reintroduce the shredded chicken to the slow cooker.
- ➢ Before serving, the soup should be seasoned with salt and black pepper, to taste.
- ➢ The chicken tortilla soup should be served hot and topped with lime wedges, chopped fresh coriander, and crushed tortilla chips.

Ingredients:

- 500 grams of skinless, boneless chicken thighs, chopped into small pieces
- 1 diced onion, 2 diced carrots, 2 diced celery stalks, 2 minced garlic cloves
- chicken stock, 4 cups
- one tablespoon of dried thyme
- Bay leaf, one
- To taste, add salt and black pepper.
- chopped fresh parsley for a garnish.

Method:

- To the slow cooker, add the following ingredients: chicken thighs, chopped onion, diced carrots, diced celery, minced garlic, dried thyme, bay leaf, salt, and black pepper. Stir to combine.
- Cover the slow cooker and simmer on low heat for six to eight hours or on high heat for three to four hours, depending on when the chicken is thoroughly cooked and soft.
- After the bay leaf has been taken out and thrown away, the soup should be served.
- The chicken pieces can be taken out of the slow cooker with a slotted spoon and placed on a cutting board. Put the chicken back in the slow cooker after shredding it with two forks.
- Add salt and freshly ground black pepper to the soup as desired. Adjust the seasoning as necessary.
- Serve the hot chicken and vegetable soup while it's still hot and sprinkle some freshly chopped parsley on top of each bowl.

CHAPTER 9
VEGETABLE

"SLOW COOKER BEANS AND POTATOES:

Ingredients:

- 250 grams of overnight soaked and drained dried beans, such as kidney, cannellini, or black beans.
- 2 diced and peeled potatoes
- 1 diced onion
- 2 minced garlic cloves
- 4 cups of chicken or vegetable stock
- one tablespoon of dried thyme
- 1 paprika teaspoon
- To taste, add salt and black pepper.
- chopped fresh parsley for a garnish.

Method:

- ➤ In the slow cooker, combine the soaked and then drained beans, diced potatoes, minced garlic, onion, chicken or vegetable stock, dried thyme, and paprika. Mix by stirring.
- ➤ Remove the lid from the slow cooker once the beans have the desired consistency, or cook them for an additional 8 to 10 hours on low heat or 4 to 6 hours on high heat.
- ➤ Before serving the beans and potatoes, season with salt and black pepper to taste.
- ➤ Add freshly chopped parsley to the top of each serving of warmed beans and potatoes.

Ingredients:

- 2 medium eggplants, 2 zucchinis, 1 red bell pepper, and 5g dried basil, all diced
- Dry oregano, 5 grams
- pepper and salt as desired
- basil leaves for garnish, fresh
- Sliced yellow bell pepper, onion, and three minced garlic cloves
- 1 tomato diced can
- Tomato paste, two tablespoons

Method:

- ➤ The diced eggplant, sliced zucchini, diced bell peppers, minced onion, and minced garlic should all be added to the Crock Pot.
- ➤ Diced tomatoes, tomato paste, dried basil, dried oregano, and a dash of salt and pepper go into a bowl to make tomato sauce. Give everything a good swirl to combine after adding the mixture and the vegetables to the slow cooker.
- ➤ The vegetables should be covered and simmered for six to eight hours at a low heat, or three to four hours at a high heat, until they are soft.
- ➤ Serve warm and, if desired, top with fresh basil leaves for a final flourish.

Ingredients:

- 1 pound of halved and trimmed Brussels sprouts
- Olive oil, two tablespoons
- pepper and salt as desired
- grated Parmesan cheese, 1/4 cup.
- Balsamic vinegar, two tablespoons
- Honey, two tablespoons

Method:

- ➤ Turn the slow cooker to low and add the Brussels sprouts.
- ➤ Combine the olive oil, honey, balsamic vinegar, salt, and pepper in a small bowl and whisk to combine. Pour the liquid over the Brussels sprouts, then toss them to distribute it evenly.
- ➤ Cook the Brussels sprouts until they are soft, covered, for three to four hours on a low heat or for one to two hours on a high heat.
- ➤ Before serving, if desired, top the prepared dish with grated Parmesan cheese.

CHAPTER 10
DESSERTS

"CROCKPOT STICKY TOFFEE MONKEY BREAD:

Ingredients:

- 500 g of white flour
- 7 grams of quick yeast
- 50 grams of sugar, caster
- 120 milliliters of warm milk and 1/2 teaspoon salt
- 60 grams of melted unsalted butter
- two huge eggs
- 100 grams of brown sugar, light
- 1 teaspoon of cinnamon powder
- 120 milliliters of double cream and 120 grams of melted unsalted butter.
- sugar demerara, 120 grams

METHOD:

- Mix together the flour, instant yeast, caster sugar, salt, and all of the above in a large bowl.
- In a different bowl, whisk the eggs, heated milk, and melted butter until thoroughly combined.
- Pour the liquid ingredients into the dry ingredients, then combine everything and stir until dough forms.
- Move the dough to a flour-dusted surface and knead it there for five to seven minutes, or until it is elastic and smooth.
- The slow cooker's interior should be greased with butter or cooking spray.
- In a bowl separate from the other ingredients, combine the ground cinnamon and light brown sugar.
- Each piece of the dough should be broken into tiny pieces before being rolled into balls.
- Each dough ball should be coated in the cinnamon sugar mixture after being dipped in the melted butter. Place the covered dough balls in the buttered slow cooker.
- In a small saucepan, heat the demerara sugar and double cream until the sugar is completely dissolved.
- Pour the cream mixture over the dough balls after you've put them in the slow cooker.
- For two to three hours, or until the bread is golden and thoroughly cooked, bake it in the Crockpot on low heat with the lid on.
- Any leftover caramel sauce from using the Crockpot should be sprinkled on the warm sticky toffee monkey bread.

Ingredients:

- 4-5 medium apples, cored, sliced, and with the peel on
- 200 g of white flour
- Sugar, caster, 150 grams
- 1 teaspoon of cinnamon powder
- 1/8 teaspoon of nutmeg, ground
- 1/4 teaspoon of cloves, ground
- A half-teaspoon of baking powder
- 1/4 teaspoon of salt
- 120 milliliters of melted milk with 120 grams of unsalted butter
- For serving, use custard or vanilla ice cream (optional)

Method:

- ➤ The slow cooker's interior should be greased with butter or cooking spray.
- ➤ Place the butter-coated, cut apples in the slow cooker.
- ➤ Before stirring them together, combine the following ingredients in a bowl: flour, caster sugar, cinnamon, nutmeg, cloves, baking powder, and salt.
- ➤ Pour the milk over the dry ingredients after the butter has melted, and stir to combine everything.
- ➤ Pour the batter over the cut apples that are already in the slow cooker after spreading it out evenly.
- ➤ For three to four hours, or until the cake is thoroughly cooked through and the apples are soft, cook the cake in the Crockpot on low heat with the lid on.
- ➤ If you'd like, you can serve vanilla ice cream or custard alongside the warm spiced apple dump cake.

CROCKPOT SALTED CARAMEL SAUCE:

Ingredients:

- 200 grams of sugar, granulated.
- 90 grams of butter, unsalted
- Double cream, 240 milliliters
- Vanilla extract, 1 teaspoon
- 50 ml of sea salt

Method:

- ➤ In a heavy-bottomed pot set over medium heat, the granulated sugar should be heated until it melts and turns amber in color. Continuous stirring should be used throughout this process.
- ➤ Put the unsalted butter in the pot and stir it to ensure that it melts and is thoroughly combined.
- ➤ Slowly stream in the double cream while stirring continuously. It is advised to exercise caution because the mixture has a chance of producing bubbles.
- ➤ Add the coarse sea salt and vanilla bean essence.
- ➤ Transferring the caramel sauce to the slow cooker is necessary.
- ➤ Cooking in a crockpot should take two to three hours on low heat with frequent stirring.
- ➤ Remove the caramel sauce from the slow cooker and let it cool after it has thickened and reached the desired consistency.
- ➤ Pour the caramel sauce into a jar or another airtight container once it has cooled.
- ➤ It will keep for up to two weeks in the refrigerator if you put the caramel sauce there.
- ➤ You can drizzle the salted caramel sauce over ice cream, desserts, or any other delectable treat of your choice.

Ingredients:

- Cans of cherry pie filling, 400 grams
- 150 grams of granulated sugar and 250 grams of self-rising flour
- Unsweetened cocoa powder in 60 grams
- A half-teaspoon of baking powder
- 240 milliliters of milk and 1/4 teaspoon salt
- 60 grams of melted unsalted butter.
- Vanilla extract, 1 teaspoon
- For serving, use whipped cream or vanilla ice cream (optional)

Method:

- ➤ Butter or nonstick cooking spray should be used to grease the slow cooker.
- ➤ The bottom of the slow cooker needs to be evenly covered with the cherry pie filling.
- ➤ The self-rising flour, granulated sugar, cocoa powder, baking soda, and salt should all be combined in a sizable mixing bowl.
- ➤ The milk, melted butter, and vanilla extract are among the liquid ingredients that should be added to the dry ingredients mixture. All of the ingredients are combined and stirred until the mixture is smooth.
- ➤ The cherry pie filling that has already been put in the Crockpot should be evenly covered with the batter.
- ➤ Cover the Crockpot and simmer on low heat for three to four hours, or until a toothpick inserted into the center of the cake comes out clean. When the cake is fully cooked, it is considered finished.
- ➤ Vanilla ice cream or whipped cream are optional toppings for the warm chocolate cherry dump cake. Serving cake at room temperature is recommended.

CHAPTER 11
SNACKS

Ingredients:

- 1.5 kilograms of fat-trimmed pork shoulder
- Brown sugar, 2 tablespoons
- Paprika, 1 tablespoon
- 10 grams of chili powder
- 5 g each of salt, cumin, garlic, and onion powder
- Black pepper, half a teaspoon
- 1/four teaspoon cayenne
- 2 tablespoons apple cider vinegar and 240 milliliters of chicken broth
- Worcestershire sauce, two tablespoons
- Tomato paste, two tablespoons
- Soft tortillas or buns for hamburgers, with Cole slaw or pickles for sprinkling (optional)

Method:

- ➤ Brown sugar, paprika, chili powder, cumin, garlic powder, onion powder, salt, black pepper, and cayenne pepper should all be combined in a small bowl to make a spice rub. Mix thoroughly.
- ➤ Rub the spice mixture all over the pork shoulder to ensure that it has been thoroughly coated.
- ➤ Turn the slow cooker to low and add the pork shoulder.
- ➤ In an additional bowl, combine the tomato paste, Worcestershire sauce, and tomato paste using a whisk.
- ➤ Over the pork shoulder that is currently in the slow cooker, pour the mixture.
- ➤ Cook the pork in the Crockpot on low heat for eight to ten hours with the lid on, or until it is tender and easily pulled apart with a fork.
- ➤ The pork ought to be shred with two forks after being taken out of the slow cooker.
- ➤ Once the pork is completely shredded, return it to the slow cooker and stir it around in the cooking liquid to evenly coat it.
- ➤ Carnitas made with pulled pork can be served on soft hamburger buns or tortillas and are sweet and spicy. Add more coleslaw or pickles if you prefer a stronger flavor.

Ingredients:

- 1.5 kilograms of fat-trimmed pork shoulder
- Brown sugar, 2 tablespoons
- paprika, 15 g
- 15 g of hot sauce
- 5 g each of salt, cumin, garlic, and onion powder
- Black pepper, half a teaspoon
- 1/four teaspoon cayenne
- Chicken broth, 240 milliliters
- apple cider vinegar, 2 tablespoons
- Worcestershire sauce, two tablespoons
- Tomato paste, two tablespoons
- tortillas or soft buns for hamburgers, for serving.
- Pickles or coleslaw as toppings (optional)

Method:

- ➢ In order to make a spice rub, combine brown sugar, paprika, chili powder, cumin, garlic powder, onion powder, salt, black pepper, and cayenne pepper in a small dish. Completely combine.
- ➢ To ensure that the pork shoulder is well coated with the seasoning and evenly distributed, rub the spice mixture all over it.
- ➢ At this point, insert the pork shoulder into the slow cooker.
- ➢ Use a whisk to combine the tomato paste, Worcestershire sauce, and tomato paste in a different bowl. The Worcestershire sauce is then added to the mixture.
- ➢ The pork shoulder should be covered in sauce after it has been added to the slow cooker and poured over.
- ➢ Depending on how tender you want your pork, it should be cooked for eight to ten hours on low heat with the lid on the slow cooker. To put it another way, it must be cooked until it is completely tender.
- ➢ Before serving, shred the pork with two forks after it has been taken out of the slow cooker.
- ➢ After you have finished shredding the pork, place it back into the slow cooker and stir it around to evenly coat it with the cooking liquid.
- ➢ If at all possible, soft tortillas or hamburger buns should be used to serve carnitas. If you want to give the dish an extra flavorful boost, add some coleslaw or pickles.

Ingredients:

- 500 g chicken breasts, skinless and without any bones
- 1 chopped onion, 2 diced carrots
- two diced celery stalks and two minced garlic cloves
- one tablespoon of dried thyme
- 1 teaspoon of rosemary, dried
- 2 liters of chicken broth
- 200 grams of egg noodles, and 1 bay leaf
- pepper and salt as desired
- freshly chopped parsley (for garnish)

Method:

- The chicken breasts, onion, carrots, celery, garlic, thyme, and rosemary should all be added to the slow cooker along with the bay leaf.
- The chicken stock needs to be poured over the ingredients already in the slow cooker.
- The chicken should be simmered in the slow cooker with the lid on for six to eight hours, or until it is thoroughly cooked and tender.
- Using two forks, remove the chicken breasts from the slow cooker and shred them into little pieces. Refill the slow cooker with the shredded chicken.
- Cook the egg noodles in the slow cooker for an additional 30 minutes on the lowest heat setting, or until they reach the desired consistency (al dente).
- Season the soup with a little salt and pepper before serving.
- Before serving, the bay leaf should be thrown away.
- Place bowls on the table before serving the chicken noodle soup, and top each one with freshly chopped parsley..

Made in United States
Troutdale, OR
10/29/2023

14122467R00051